Social Justice All Around Us

Anti-Bias Learning: Social Justice in Action

By Adrienne van der Valk

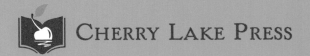

CHERRY LAKE PRESS

Published in the United States of America by Cherry Lake Publishing Group
Ann Arbor, Michigan
www.cherrylakepublishing.com

Developed with help from Learning for Justice, a project of the Southern Poverty Law Center. With special
thanks to Monita Bell and Hoyt Phillips.
Reading Adviser: Beth Walker Gambro, MS, Ed., Reading Consultant, Yorkville, IL

Photo Credits: © Brocreative/Shutterstock.com, cover, 1; © Lorena Fernandez/Shutterstock.com, 4; © Ryan
DeBerardinis/Shutterstock.com, 6; © Earth Polychromatic Imaging Camera/NASA, 8; © Melissa Hani/
Shutterstock.com, 10; © ccpixx photography/Shutterstock.com, 12; © Steve Sanchez Photos/Shutterstock.
com, 14; © Valentin Valkov/Shutterstock.com, 16; © lev radin/Shutterstock.com, 18; © Lucky Business/
Shutterstock.com, 20

Library of Congress Cataloging-in-Publication Data has been filed and is available at catalog.loc.gov

Cherry Lake Publishing Group would like to acknowledge the work of the Partnership for 21st Century Learning,
a Network of Battelle for Kids. Please visit http://www.battelleforkids.org/networks/p21 for more information.

Printed in the United States of America
Corporate Graphics

CONTENTS

5 Fairness

9 Climate Change

13 Action for the Environment

17 Sports and You

19 Equal Pay!

22 Glossary

23 Find Out More

24 Index

24 About the Author

Sharing classroom supplies or toys means everyone gets a fair turn.

Fairness

How do you know when things are fair or unfair? Do you feel it in your body? Do you think it in your mind? How else do you know? You might think about fairness when you and your friends take turns on the playground, share toys, or count your candy at Halloween. Who gets to go first? Who has more?

People might face unfairness because of the groups they belong to.
Your gender, your race, your religion, or where you live
could all affect how you are treated.

Sharing toys and taking turns are examples of fairness between **individual** people. But fairness also matters to groups of people. **Social justice** means fairness for groups of people. Social justice and **injustice** are all around us, even in places we might not expect it.

Did you know that the way we experience the weather can be a social justice issue? Even the **opportunity** to play sports can be a social justice issue. We can find chances to be fairer and more just everywhere.

Climate change is the change in the Earth's average weather and temperature due to human activity. Climate change means hotter temperatures and more extreme weather around the world.

Climate Change

Climate change is a global problem. Humans are **diverse**. We look different, speak different languages, and live different **lifestyles**. Some people live in cities and work in big buildings. Some people live on farms and raise crops and animals for food. Some people live near the ocean and feed their families by fishing.

Think!

List all the things you know about climate change. Ask yourself, "What do I want to know about climate change? How could I find out more?"

Warmer waters can mean fish have to change their habitat.
What problems might this mean for fishers?

It might seem like the weather would affect everyone the same, but it doesn't. Your **identity** has a big influence on how and when climate change will affect you. For people like farmers and fishers who depend on nature for their food, climate change is already a big problem. It's a big problem for many animals too!

Make a Guess!

Where you live influences how quickly climate change will affect you. Where do the people most hurt by climate change live?

Climate change can lead to extreme storms and flooding.

Action for the Environment

The people who have the power to stop climate change aren't the same people who are most hurt by it. The people who are most hurt by it don't own factories. Many of them don't live in cities. When people with the power to stop climate change don't listen to the people it hurts, that is an injustice.

People in New York City in 2020 march for racial and climate justice.

A lot of people around the world are angry and worried about climate change. What do they do to make their voices heard? They take action! They make signs and march in the street. They refuse to buy products from companies that make the worst **pollution**. They tell each other to vote for leaders who care about climate change.

Create!

Imagine you are attending a march to stop climate change. What would your sign say?

What do the athletes you watch on TV have in common?

Sports and You

Do you play or watch sports? Do people in your family or neighborhood play or watch sports? Are sports an important part of your identity? If so, why do you think that is? If not, why do you think it isn't?

What identities do you see most often when you watch sports teams on TV? What identities do you not see? For example, when is the last time you saw someone who had a **disability** play sports on TV? Are sports teams diverse or not? Why?

The U.S. women's soccer team has won the World Cup
four times—more than any other team in the world.

Equal Pay!

Did you know that most women athletes are paid less than men for playing the same sport? Does that seem fair to you? Many women athletes and sports fans feel that this is an injustice. They want all athletes to be paid equally for doing the same job.

Some of these athletes are members of the U.S. women's soccer team. They are taking action. They filed a **lawsuit** to say that their pay was unfair. Even their fans are speaking up. In 2019, the team

How can you stand up to injustice in your life?

won the World Cup championship. At the game, people in the stands chanted, "Equal pay!" to show their support.

Now that you have read about identity, diversity, justice, and action, you may start seeing them all around you. What examples can you think of in your own life?

Ask Questions!

What do the people in your family and community think about unequal pay? Are they only worried about unequal pay in sports?

GLOSSARY

climate change (KLY-muht CHAYNJ) long-lasting change in Earth's temperatures and weather patterns

disability (dis-uh-BIH-luh-tee) a condition that can make it more difficult for a person to do something

diverse (dye-VUHRS) varied or differing from one another

identity (eye-DEN-tuh-tee) who you are

individual (in-duh-VIJ-ooh-uhl) single and separate

injustice (in-JUH-stuhss) unfair treatment

lawsuit (LAH-soot) a legal action brought against a person or group

lifestyles (LYF-stiles) ways of living

opportunity (ah-poor-TOON-uh-tee) the chance to do something or progress in something

pollution (puh-LOO-shuhn) harmful materials that damage the air, water, and land

social justice (SOH-shuhl JUH-stuhss) fairness for groups of people

FIND OUT MORE

WEBSITES

Learning for Justice Classroom Resources—Students texts, tasks, and more
https://www.learningforjustice.org/classroom-resources

Learning for Justice—Learn more about anti-bias work and find the full Social Justice Standards framework
https://www.learningforjustice.org

Social Justice Books—Booklists and a guide for selecting anti-bias children's books
https://socialjusticebooks.org

Welcoming Schools—Creating safe and welcoming schools
https://www.welcomingschools.org

INDEX

A
air pollution, 12
animals, 9, 11
athletes, 16–17
  equal pay, 19,
    20–21
  women, 19,
    20–21

C
cities, 9, 12–13
climate change,
    7, 8–11
  action, 12–15
  anger about, 15
  who is hurt by it,
    13
climate justice, 14

D
disabilities, 17
diversity, 9
  and sports, 17

E
environment
  action for,
    12–15
equal pay, 19,
    20–21
exhaust, car, 12

F
factories, 13
fairness, 4–7
farmers, 9, 11
fish, 10
fishers, 9, 11

G
gender, 6
groups
  and fairness,
    6–7

H
habitats, fish, 10
human activity, 8

I
identity
  and climate
    change, 11
  and sports, 17
individuals
  and fairness, 7
injustice, 7, 13

J
justice, 14

L
lifestyles, 9
living environment,
    6

P
pay, equal, 19,
    20–21
pollution, 12, 15

R
race, 6
racial justice, 14
religion, 6

S
sharing, 5, 7
smog, 12
soccer, 18–19, 21
social justice, 7
sports, 7, 16–17
  and diversity, 17
  and equal pay,
    19, 20–21

T
taking turns, 5, 7
temperature,
  Earth's, 8

U
unfairness, 5, 6
U.S. women's
  soccer team,
    18–19, 21

W
waters, warmer, 10
weather, 7, 8, 11
women athletes,
    18–21
World Cup
  championship,
    18–21

ABOUT THE AUTHOR

Adrienne van der Valk is a writer, editor, podcaster, and yoga and meditation teacher. Her background is in journalism and political science, and she is passionate about issues related to racial and gender equity. She lives in the New York City area.